MW01045160

ONE

MEMENTO MORI

AND DEPICTIONS OF DEATH

AN IMAGE ARCHIVE FOR
ARTISTS *And* DESIGNERS

INTRODUCTION

VAULT EDITIONS

Memento Mori and Depictions of Death: An Image Archive for Artists and Designers by Vault Editions is a brilliantly curated pictorial archive of images exploring arguably one of the most compelling tropes in art, the inevitability of death.

This book features an extensive range of 17th and 18th-century etchings and engravings of memento mori artworks and symbolism, the Grim Reaper, death, scenes of war and execution, corpses and much more.

Features:
Each book comes with a unique download link providing instant access to high-resolution files of all images featured. These images can be used in art and graphic design projects or printed and framed to make stunning decorative artworks. We promise you will be impressed with this pictorial archive.

About the author:
This book was curated and authored by the creative director of Vault Editions, Kale James. Kale has published over 30 acclaimed books within the art design space and has worked with brands including Nike, Samsung, Adidas and Rolling Stone. Kale's artwork is published in numerous titles, including No Cure, Semi-Permanent, Vogue and more.

This collection of vintage illustrations is an essential resource for all artists, collage artists, graphic designers and tatooists looking to take their artwork to the next level.

WHAT IS A MEMENTO MORI?

The artistic trope Memento mori (Latin for 'remember that you [have to] die') is a symbolic reminder of the inevitability of death. The origins of the concept have been traced back to early Christianity, Judaism and classical antiquity. The most common symbol used in memento mori is a human skull. However, it is not uncommon to see an hourglass, wilted flowers, a winged reaper, or a coffin to symbolise life's impermanent and transient nature. These symbols were used in works of art, including portraits, where the trope was not the primary subject matter. Vanitas, on the other hand, is a genre of art that evokes the trope more directly. The primary subject matter of vanitas is death, often contrasting symbols of death, wealth and ephemerality. A vanitas is a symbolic work of art illustrating the futility of earthly pleasures, the transient nature of life, and death's certainty.

DOWNLOAD YOUR FILES

Downloading your files is simple. To access your digital files, please go to the last page of this book and follow the instructions.

For technical assistance, please email:
info@vaulteditions.com

Bibliographical Note

This book is a new work created by Vault Editions Ltd.

ISBN: 978-1-925968-78-1

MEMENTO MORI & DEPICTIONS OF DEATH

VAULT EDITIONS

MEMENTO MORI & DEPICTIONS OF DEATH

01: Bust of half a skeleton and half a young
woman, anonymous, 1615 – 1664.

02: Title print with a skull and an hourglass,
Hendrick Hondius (I), 1626.

MEMENTO MORI & DEPICTIONS
OF DEATH

04: Death with Arrow and Hourglass, Jan van de
Velde (II), 1633.

MEMENTO MORI & DEPICTIONS OF DEATH

QVIS EVADET?

Momento breuis hæc, certæ obnoxia morti
Vita, quasi fumus, bullula, flosæ perit.
Cur ergo teneris (pròh stulti) fidimus añis?
Cur non sponte mori difcimus ante diem?

Excuffa blandæ carnis, dum vita fuperftes,
Compede, post mortem liberiore gradu
Spiritus astra petet, iam fedem vbi fixerat ante
Ciuemæ agnofcet cælica turba fuum.

QVIS EVADET?

HG

Flos nouus, et verna fragrans argenteus aura
Marcescit subitò, perit, ali, perit illa venustas.
Sic et vita hominum iam nunc nascentibus, eheu,
Instar abit bullæ vaniq̃ elapsa vaporis.

F. Estius

MEMENTO MORI & DEPICTIONS
OF DEATH

06: Homo bulla, Hendrick Goltzius, 1594.

07: Life and Death, Thomas Dusart, after Werner van den Valckert, 1619.

MEMENTO MORI & DEPICTIONS
OF DEATH

08: Memento mori, Raphaël Sadeler (I), after
Christoph Schwarz, 1687 – 1749.

09

10

09: Allegory of Death, Florens Schuyl, 1629 – 1669.

10: Sleeping Child Reclining on a Skull, Barthel Beham, 1525.

11

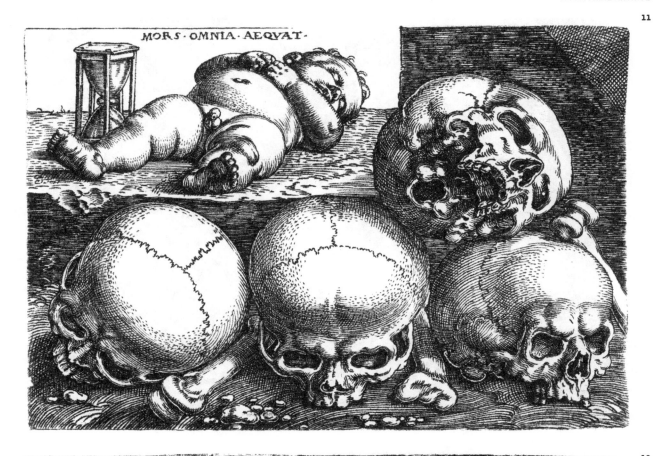

MORS·OMNIA·AEQVAT·

12

11: Sleeping Child with Hourglass and Four
Skulls, Barthel Beham, 1512 – 1540.

12: Child with three skulls, Barthel Beham, 1529.

13

14

13: Child with Skull (Vanitas), Simon van de
Passe, after Crispijn van de Passe (I), 1612.

14: Allegory of Transience, Raphaël Sadeler (I),
after Maerten de Vos, 1570 – 1632.

15: Impermanence, Heinrich Aldegrever, after
Albrecht Dürer, 1529.

16

17

18

19

16: Abbess and Death, Rudolph Meyer, 1650.   17: Abbot and Death, Rudolph Meyer, 1650.   18: Architect and Death, Rudolph Meyer, 1650.   19: Astrologer and Death, Conrad Meyer, after
Rudolph Meyer, 1650.

20

21

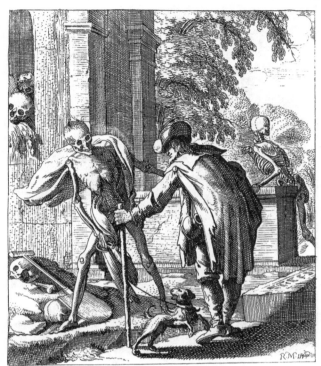

22

23

20: Beggars and Death, Rudolph Meyer, 1650.　　21: Blind Man and Death, Rudolph Meyer, 1650.　　22: Charlatan and Death, Rudolph Meyer, 1650.　　23: Child and Death, Conrad Meyer, after Rudolph Meyer, 1650.

24

25

26

27

MEMENTO MORI & DEPICTIONS OF DEATH

24: Death and a Young Man, Johann Theodor de Bry, after Crispijn van de Passe, 1596

25: Death Comes to Collect Beauty, Johann Theodor de Bry, 1596.

26: Death Penalty, Rudolph Meyer, 1650.

27: Doctor and Death, Conrad Meyer, after Rudolph Meyer, 1650.

28

29

30

31

28: Earl and Countess and Death, Rudolph
Meyer, 1650.

29: King and Death, Rudolph Meyer, 1650.

30: Knight and Death, Conrad Meyer, 1650.

31: Lovers and Death, Rudolph Meyer, 1650.

32

33

34

35

32: Man and Woman with Death, Rudolph Meyer, 1650.   33: Merchant and Death, Conrad Meyer, 1650.   34: Merchant and Death, Rudolph Meyer, 1650.   35: Peddler and Death, Conrad Meyer, after Rudolph Meyer, 1650.

36

37

38

39

36: Queen and Death, Rudolph Meyer, 1650.   37: Triumph of Death, Conrad Meyer, after Rudolph Meyer, 1650.   38: Uncertainty of Death, Rudolph Meyer, 1650.   39: Usurer and Death, Conrad Meyer, 1650.

40: The Horrors of War, Number 7, Gottfried
Bernhard Götz, 1742.

MEMENTO MORI & DEPICTIONS OF DEATH

41: The Horrors of War, Number 4, Gottfried
Bernhard Götz, 1742.

42

42: Death plays music between dead actors,
Gustav Richard Steinbrecher, Alfred Rethel, 1851.

43

43: Death Tolls the Bell, Richard Julius Jungtow,
Alfred Rethel, 1851.

44

44: Usurer and Death, Conrad Meyer, 1650.

MEMENTO MORI & DEPICTIONS OF DEATH

45: Death of Adam and Eve, Jan Ditmaer, after
Crispijn van den Broeck, 1548 – 1603.

46

47

46: Young Couple and Death, Werner van den Valckert, 1610 – 1612.

47: Couple Surprised by Death, Frans Menton, after Angelo Speeck, 1568.

48: Death with a cape, a scythe and
an hourglass amid human bones, Isaac
Weissenbruch, 1836 – 1912.

49

50

51

52

49: Victory over Death, anonymous, after
Hendrick Goltzius, 1601 – 1667.

50: Soldier and Death, Rudolph Meyer, 1650.

51: Hermit and Death, Conrad Meyer, after
Rudolph Meyer, 1650.

52: Nobleman and Death, Conrad Meyer, 1650.

53

54

53: Procession of the Dead, Pieter van der Borcht (I), 1558 – 1619.

54: Old woman with two skeletons at a table, anonymous, after Adriaen Brouwer, 1622 – 1688.

55: Title print for print series De masquerades,
Jacob de Gheyn (II), 1595 – 1596.

56: Death and Fama, Rudolph Meyer, 1650.

57

58

57: Raising the Dead, Hendrick Goltzius, after
Jan van der Straet, 1575 – 1579.

58: Man at the age of ninety, Crispijn van de
Passe (I), 1574 – 1637.

60

59: Title print for print series The Riding School,
Jacob de Gheyn (II), 1599.

60: Tablets of the law, weaponry and ornament
with skulls, Bernard Picart, 1683 – 1733.

MEMENTO MORI & DEPICTIONS
OF DEATH

61: Christ as Shield and Helmet, anonymous, c.
1579 – c. 1615.

62: God Separates Light and Dark, Bernard
Picart, 1683 – 1733.

63: Vignette with the Personification of Death,
Jacob Folkema, after Johannes de Bosch, 1741.

64

65

64: Vanitas still life, Willem Steelink (II), after
Pieter Claesz., 1888 – 1891.

65: Vanitas Still Life with a Skull with Laurel
Wreath, Hendrick Hondius (I), 1626.

68

66: Vanitas with globe, crucifix, skull and books, Jan Matham, after Jacob Matham, 1628 – 1648.

67: Putto with skull, Crispijn van de Passe (I), 1594.

68: Vanitas Symbols, Daniel Nikolaus Chodowiecki, 1770.

69

ETIAM FEROCISSIMOS DOMARI
PER FEROCE CHE SIA CONVIEN ESSER DOMATO

Venetijs luca Bertelli formis.

69: Armed Skeleton, Allegory of Death, Luca
Bertelli, after Titiaan, c. 1565.

71

70: Amor and Death, as Skeleton with Spear,
Henricus Wilhelmus Couwenberg, 1830 – 1845.

71: Vignette with Death and a Putto, Reinier
Vinkeles (I), 1751 – 1816.

72

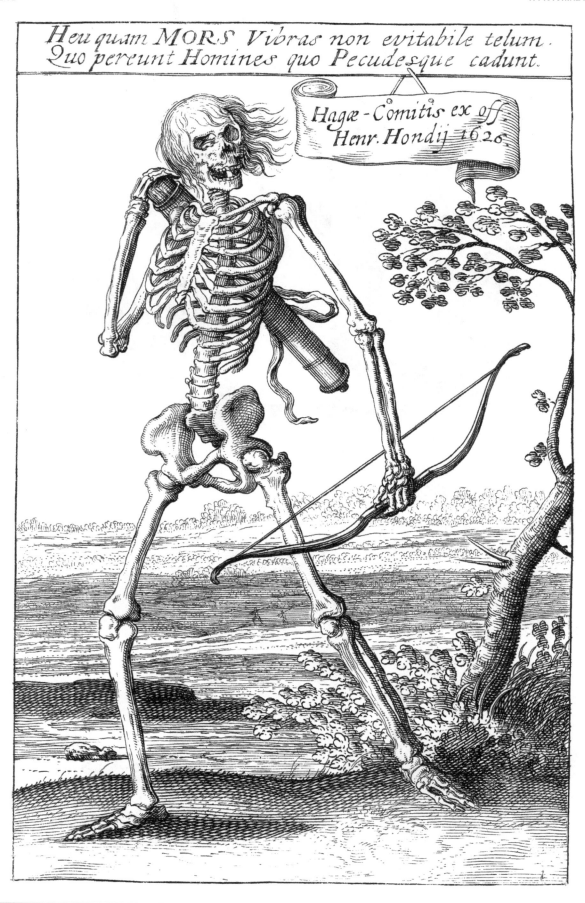

72: Skeleton with Bow and Arrow, Hendrick
Hondius, after Teodoro Filippo di Liagno, 1626.

73: Skeleton bust, Egbert van Panderen, after
Joannes Bernardinus S., c. 1590 – 1637.

74

74: Skeleton with banner, Hendrick Hondius,
after Teodoro Filippo di Liagno, 1625 – 1652.

75

76

75: Skull cartouche, Hendrick Hondius (I)
(rejected attribution), 1649.

76: Two Fighting Men and Death, anonymous,
after Jan Lievens, 1617 – 1699.

77

77: The Triumph of Death, Boëtius Adamsz.
Bolswert, after David Vinckboons (1), 1610.

79: City dwellers and peasants look at two skeletons and an angel with a book
open at the depiction of the last judgement, Cornelis van Dalen (II), 1659.

80: Human skeleton reads a list of animal names,
Jan Luyken, 1680.

MEMENTO MORI & DEPICTIONS OF DEATH

81: Allegory of Death, Raphaël Sadeler (I), 1617.

82: Allegory of Transience (Vanitas), Hieronymus
Wierix, 1563 – before 1619.

MEMENTO MORI & DEPICTIONS
OF DEATH

83: Father Time and Transience, Coenraet
Decker, 1672 – 1676.

MEMENTO MORI & DEPICTIONS OF DEATH

84: Allegory of the Vanity (Death and the Girl), Andries Jacobsz. Stock (attributed to), after Jacob de Gheyn (II), 1608 – 1612.

85

S. F. inv. et fec.

85: Death, Simon Fokke, 1722 – 1784.

86: Child in the Skeleton of Death, Boëtius
Adamsz. Bolswert, 1624.

87

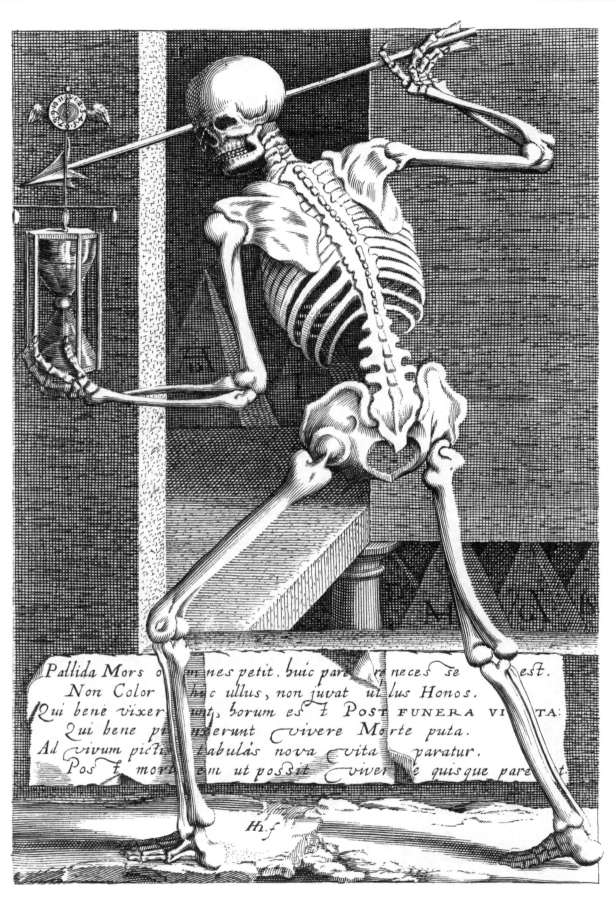

87: Death with an Hourglass and an Arrow,
Hendrick Hondius (I), 1610.

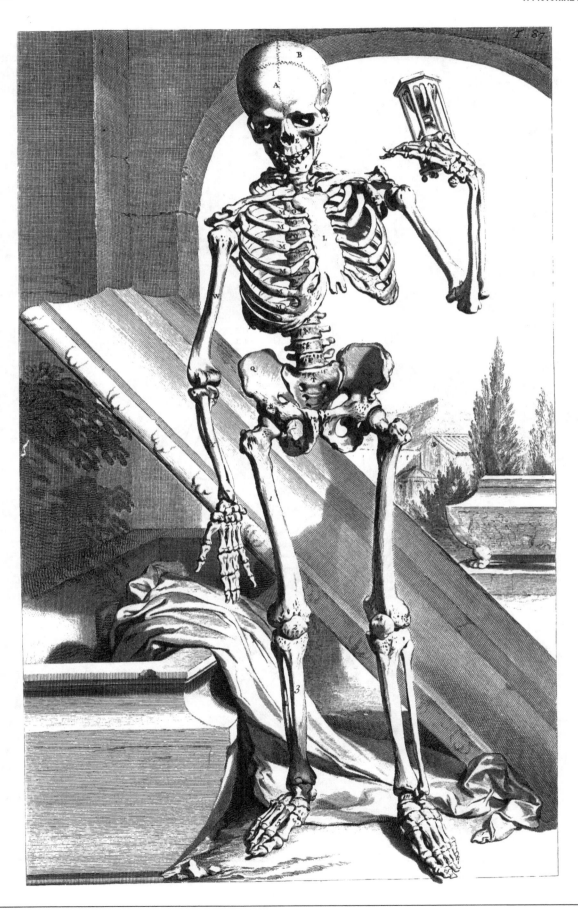

MEMENTO MORI & DEPICTIONS OF DEATH

88: Anatomical skeleton of a human holding an hour glass.

MEMENTO MORI & DEPICTIONS OF DEATH

90: Mirror of Human Life, Marcello Clodio, c. 1598.

91: Death as a reaper with a scythe, anonymous,
1600 – 1699.

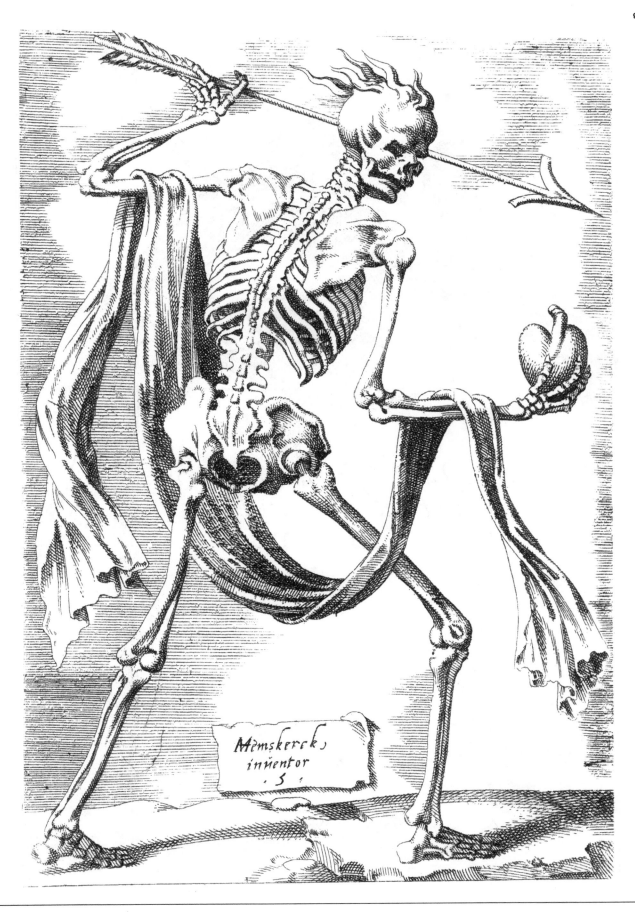

Memskerck, inuentor .5.

92: Death of sin brings a new person to life, Dirck Volckertsz.
Coornhert, after Maarten van Heemskerck, 1550.

93

MEMENTO MORI & DEPICTIONS
OF DEATH

Quis est homo qui vi-
vet et non videbit
MORTEM.
PS. 88.

Hagæ-Comitis
ex Officina H. hondius
1642.

93: Winged Skeleton with Hourglass on a
Tombstone, Hendrick Hondius, 1642.

95

95: Young Man with Skull, Jan Harmensz. Muller
(manner or), 1598 – 1612.

96: Young Man with a Skull, Lucas van Leyden,
1517 – 1521.

97

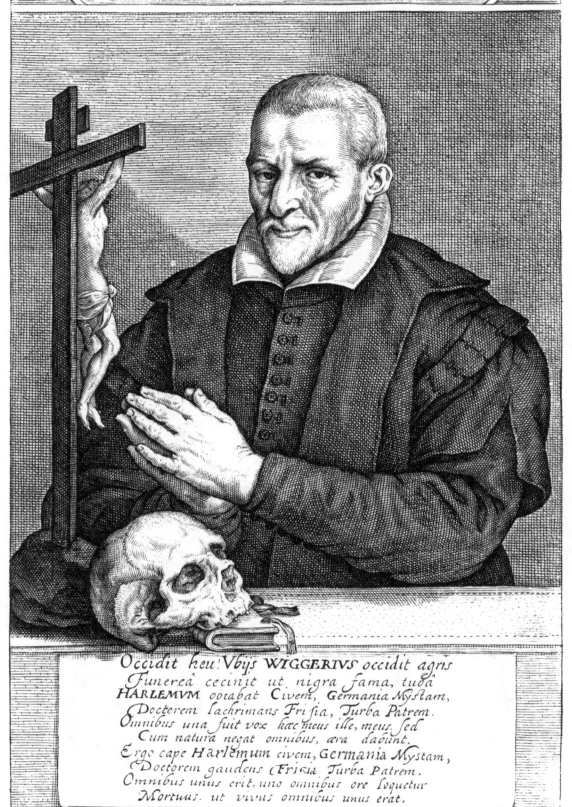

R. D. Mr. NICOLAVS WIGGERIVS
OBIIT VIII. KAL. APRIL. A: cɪɔ. ɪɔc. XXVIII ÆTATIS
LXXII. SACERDOTH XLVII ORDINIS XXV.

Soutman
pinxit

Matham
sculpsit

Occidit heu! Vbys WIGGERIVS occidit agris
Funereâ cecinit ut nigra fama, tubâ
HARLEMVM optabat Civem, Germania Mystam,
Doctorem lachrimans Frisia, Turba Patrem.
Omnibus una fuit vox hæc meus ille, meus sed
Cum natura negat omnibus, æra dabunt.
Ergo cape Harlemum civem, Germania Mystam,
Doctorem gaudens (Frisia Turba Patrem.
Omnibus unus erit, uno omnibus ore loquetur
Mortuus, ut vivus omnibus unus erat.

97: Portrait of Claes Wiggers Cousebant Vigerius,
Jacob Matham, after Pieter Claesz. Soutman, 1628.

Le veritable portrait de la bien heureuse Marguerite de Lorraine petite
fille de René de france Roy de sicile et d'Arragon, Niepce de Marguerite de france
Royne d'Angleterre; Vefue de Monseig.r René de france duc d'Allençon, mere de Charles
dernier duc d'Allençon, et de françoise d'allençon, ayeulle d'Anthoine Roy de Nauarre,
pere de Henry le Grand Roy de france et de Nauarre, et trisayeulle des dessendas
dud.t Henry le Grand. Fondatrice de plusieurs Monasteres de filles de lordre de
S.te Claire Laquelle est morte Religieuse en celuy d'Argenten. le deux Nouem-
bre 1521. ou son corps est encor entier.

Van schuppen faciebat octob.r An.o 1660

99: Portrait of monk F.J. van der Linden with skull, Nicolas
van den Bergh, after Peter Paul Rubens, 1735 – 1774.

100: Portrait of Gideon Harvey, Pieter Philippe,
1663.

MEMENTO MORI & DEPICTIONS
OF DEATH

VINCE
TE
IPSVM.

P.Holsteyn Sculp.

101: Portrait of Joannes Wier, Pieter Holsteyn
(II), 1660.

102: Portrait of Jan Neyen, Jan Harmensz. Muller,
after Michiel Jansz van Miereveit, 1608.

103: Portrait of Heinrich Meene at the age of 35,
Christian Fritzsch, after Gottfried Sporleder, 1746.

VITA VT FLOS FVGAX
ERGO
DISCE MORI

104: Portrait of Michael Rötenbeck, Hans
Troschel, 1623 – 1628.

105

105: Portrait of Fernando Alvarez de Toledo, Duke of Alba, Pieter
van Gunst, after Adriaen van der Werff, c. 1669 – 1731.

106

107

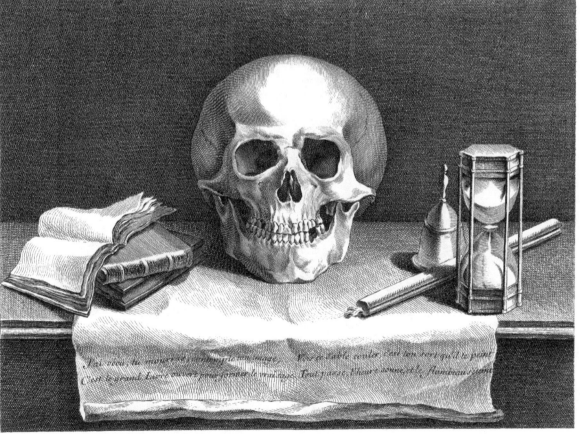

106: Death of Seneca, Simon Francois Ravenet
(le vieux), 1768.

107: Still life with vanitas symbols, Jean Aubert,
after Edme Bouchardon, 1708 – 1741.

B.IOANNES CHISIVS.

Ord. Eremit.S.Augustini, Nobili Chisiorum
genere ortus, Religiosa castitatis aliarumq
virtutum exemplar singulare obijt A.1363.

108: Portrait of Beato Giovanni Chigi, anonymous,
after Abraham van Diepenbeeck, 1622 – 1725.

109: Title print with title on an urn, Giovanni
Battista Piranesi, c. 1756 – c. 1757.

110

MEMENTO MORI & DEPICTIONS OF DEATH

111

110: Couple Threatened by Father Time and
Death, Hieronymus Wierix, 1563 – before 1619.

111: Woman with a comb looks into a mirror,
Alexander Voet (II), 1661 – 1695.

112: Melancholie, Simon Henri Thomassin, after
Domenico Feti, 1729 – c. 1740.

MEMENTO MORI & DEPICTIONS OF DEATH

114: Penitent Mary Magdalene, Hendrick
Goltzius, 1595 – 1599.

115

115: Saint Jerome of Bethlehem as Hermit, Boëtius Adamsz.
Bolswert, after Abraham Bloemaert, 1590 – 1612.

B. Sprangers iv.
I. Sadeler? scalps

116: Saint Jerome, Johann Sadeler (I), after
Bartholomeus Spranger, 1560 – 1600.

117: Saint Jerome, Agostino Carracci, after
Francesco Vanni, c. 1595.

118: Self—portrait with skull and bowl, Jacob
Binck, 1510 – 1569.

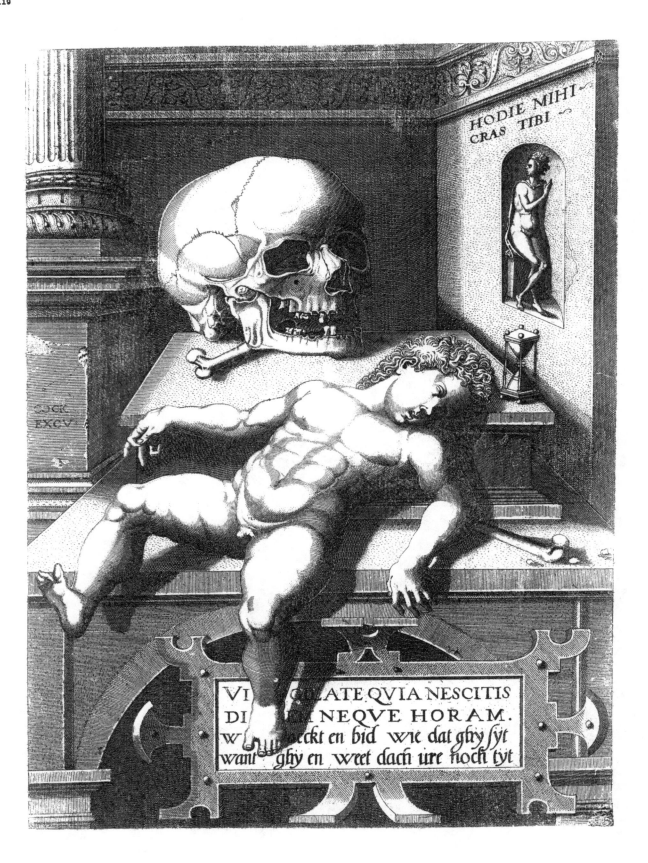

119: Vanitas depiction with child and skull,
Hieronymus Cock, after anonymous, c. 1550.

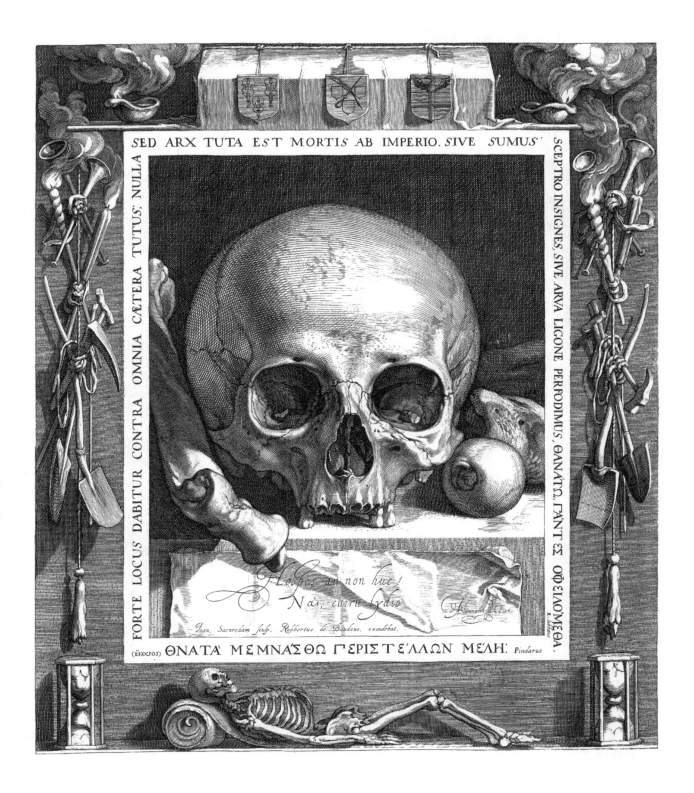

120: Vanitas still life with skull, Jan Saenredam,
after Abraham Bloemaert, 1575 – 1607.

MEMENTO MORI & DEPICTIONS OF DEATH

121: Grieving Philosopher Surrounded by Vanitas Symbolism,
Gabriel Ehinger, after Johann Heinrich Schönfeld, 1652 – 1736.

122: Reclining Putto with Hourglass and Skull,
Zacharias Dolendo, c. 1580 – c. 1601.

123: Penitent Mary Magdalene in a Cave, Lucas
Vorsterman (I), 1619 – 1675.

124

124: Martyrdom of Henricus Turck, Gaspar
Bouttats, 1650 – 1695.

MEMENTO MORI & DEPICTIONS
OF DEATH

125: Martyrdom of Jesuit Carlo Spinola at Nagasaki,
Schelte Adamsz. Bolswert, 1596 – 1659.

126

126: Man Who Blasphemed God's Name Is Stoned, Abraham de
Blois, after Gerard Hoet (I), 1720 – 1728.

MEMENTO MORI & DEPICTIONS
OF DEATH

127: The Elders Are Stoned, Heinrich Aldegrever,
1555.

MEMENTO MORI & DEPICTIONS
OF DEATH

128: Adam and Eve at the Corpse of Abel, Carlo Antonio
Porporati, after Adriaen van der Werff, 1776.

129: Adam and Eve mourn the death of Abel, Jan
Saenredam, after Abraham Bloemaert, 1604.

130

130: Pieta, Hieronymus Wierix, after Taddeo
Zuccaro, 1563 – before 1580.

MEMENTO MORI & DEPICTIONS
OF DEATH

131: Holy Trinity and Angels with Instruments of Suffering, Schelte
Adamsz. Bolswert, after Peter Paul Rubens, 1596 – 1659.

132

133

MEMENTO MORI & DEPICTIONS OF DEATH

132: Body of the Dead Christ, Paulus Pontius,
after Abraham van Diepenbeeck, 1616 – 1657.

133: Second Coming of Christ, Rudolph Meyer,
1650.

134

135

134: Lamentation, Jean Pesne, after Nicolas
Poussin, 1640 – 1700.

135: The Raising of Tabita by the Apostle Peter, Cornelis
Bloemaert (II), after Guercino, 1664 – 1692.

136: Whoever kills lust and lies is praised by truth, Dirck Volckertsz.
Coornhert, after Adriaan de Weerdt, 1566 – 1578.

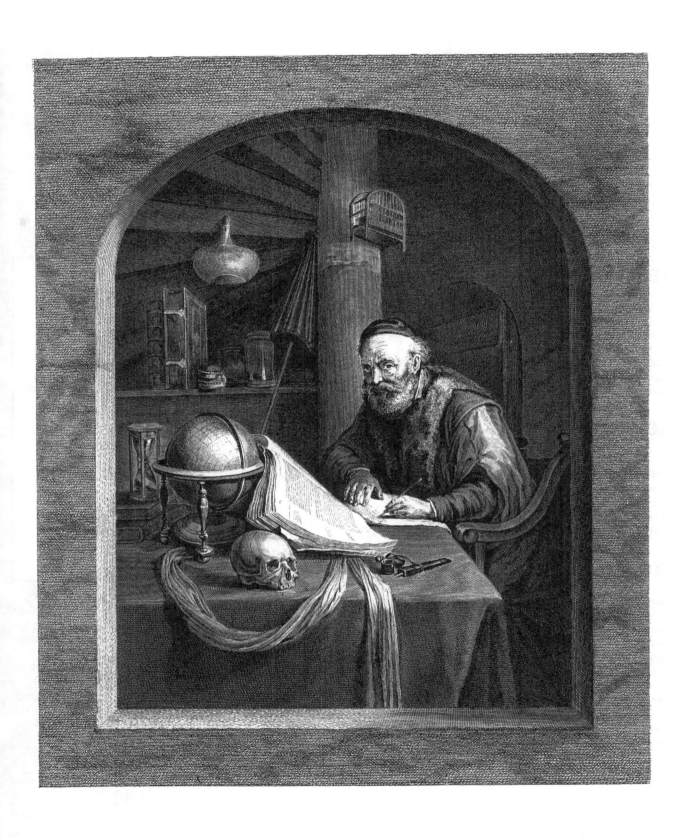

137: Scholar in his Study, Writing at a Table, Nicolas
Joseph Voyez, after Gerard Dou, 1752 – 1797.

LEARN MORE

At Vault Editions, our mission is to create the world's most diverse and comprehensive collection of image archives available for artists, designers and curious minds. If you have enjoyed this book, you can find more of our titles available at vaulteditions.com.

REVIEW THIS BOOK

As a small, family-owned independent publisher, reviews help spread the word about our work. We would be incredibly grateful if you could leave an honest review of this title wherever you purchased this book.

JOIN OUR COMMUNITY

Are you a creative and curious individual? If so, you will love our community on Instagram. Every day we share bizarre and beautiful artwork ranging from 17th and 18th-century natural history and scientific illustration, to mythical beasts, ornamental designs, anatomical illustration and more. Join our community of 100K+ people today—search @vault_editions on Instagram.

DOWNLOAD YOUR FILES

STEP ONE

Enter the following web address in your web browser on a desktop computer.

www.vaulteditions.com/mma

STEP TWO

Enter the following unique password to access the download page.

mma384536fsctrx2

STEP THREE

Follow the prompts to access your high-resolution files.

TECHNICAL ASSISTANCE

For all technical assistance, please email: info@vaulteditions.com

Made in United States
Troutdale, OR
01/27/2024

17163208R00058